Minibeasts

By Sandy Green   Photography by Chris Fairclough

Contents

FRANKLIN WATTS

LONDON·SYDNEY

A minibeast hunt

Minibeasts can be found everywhere. How many different types can you find in your garden or outdoor classroom?

Explore different areas. Look under stones and logs. Try digging the soil.

How many worms were there?

How many snails?

How many woodlice?

What else did you find?

Make a record of all the minibeasts you have found.

We found that everyone's chart was a bit different.

3

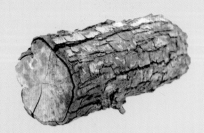

Build a home for a minibeast

Talk about the different places minibeasts like to live, such as under logs and stones, in the soil and in bushes.

- Choose your favourite minibeast and build a home for it.

- Does your minibeast prefer light or shade?

Woodlouse

- Find everything that you need.

- Build your home in a suitable place.

Woodlice will love living here.

5

Make a ladybird shelter

Make a shelter for ladybirds.

Ladybird

- Watch where ladybirds like to go and which plants are their favourite. This will help you decide where to put your shelter.

- Find and collect sticks about as thick as your finger.

- Tie the sticks together in bundles.

- Have a look at your shelter as often as you can. Have you seen any ladybirds visit your shelter yet?

Have you counted the spots on the ladybirds? How many were there? Are there always the same number?

Get up close to minibeasts

Many minibeasts are quite small and can be hard to see clearly.

Magnifying glasses help you look at them in more detail.

Count the legs on a woodlouse or beetle. How many did you count? Which minibeast has the most legs?

Glossary: **magnifying glass** – a piece of glass that makes small things look bigger.

- Look at the markings on worms and snails.

- Draw pictures of the minibeasts you like the best.

Observe snails

- Collect some snails to look at.

- Put them in an old fish tank with grass, stones and pieces of wood.

- Put some leaves in for them to nibble.

- Use a magnifying glass to look at their horns (tentacles).

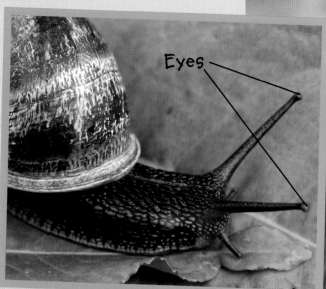

Eyes

The large horns have eyes. Can you see them? The smallest horns are for smelling.

- As the snail climbs the side of the tank, watch it move on its one large squishy foot.

- How long does it take to reach the top?

Remember to put the snails back where you found them.

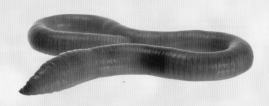

Make a wormery

Worms wriggle through the soil, mixing it up as they move around.

Use some coloured sand

- Observe their movements by making a wormery.

- Use a clear box or jar and fill it with layers of soil and sand.

- Carefully dig up some worms and put them in your wormery.

- Put on a lid with holes in it to let air in. Cover the sides with black paper to keep it dark.

- Have a look each day.

- Remember to keep the soil damp and to put the worms back where you found them after a few days.

How long does it take for the worms to mix the soil and sand together, just like in the garden?

What's in the pond?

Sit quietly by a pond, and just listen. What can you hear?

Soon you will start to identify sounds.

You will probably hear flies buzzing, or the plop, plop sound of tiny insects landing in the water and fishes coming up to eat them.

Glossary: **identify** – work out what something is.

The breeze makes the plant life rustle. You may hear a frog croaking.

You might see dragonflies and damselflies, too, but you probably won't hear them. Why do you think this might be?

Pond dipping

Stand carefully on the edge of a pond to dip your net.

Pond dipping is when you use nets with long handles to find out what is in a pond or stream.

Sometimes you can put wellies on and stand in a stream with your net.

What did you catch? Have you found any pond skaters or water snails?

Pond skater

Water snail

Dragonfly larvae

- Tip your net into a white or yellow tray filled with water and look at the contents closely.

- Remember to tip everything back afterwards.

It is important to always keep yourself safe by water. Always have an adult nearby. Stand still and never run or push anyone.

A frog's life cycle

Is there any frogspawn on your pond? If not, ask a friend with a pond nearby if they have some to spare and put it in your pond.

Frogspawn looks like glue with black spots.

Soon you will see that the spots have tails. They are now called tadpoles.

Tiny legs soon grow.

At last the tails will go and the tadpoles become frogs.

After three years the frogs will make more frogspawn, and more frogs will develop. This is called a life cycle.

Draw a picture of each stage of the life cycle of a frog. Label each stage.

Make your own minibeast

Make your own minibeast using natural materials.
Look for twigs, leaves, bark and flowers.

Tie the materials together if you want to hang them up, or you can just build them on the ground.

How many legs will it have? What will you call your minibeast?

This minibeast is called a bobble-eye. It has buttercup eyes on a body made from bark, pine cones and leaves.

Activity ideas

A minibeast hunt (pages 2-3)
- Talk about what is a minibeast and how they differ from other types of creatures.
- Talk about the importance of handling minibeasts carefully and of making sure they have food and shelter if being kept for observation.
- Emphasise the importance of putting minibeasts back where they were found.

Build a home for a minibeast (pages 4-5)
- Try making a chart with the children of which minibeasts live where.
- Explore your garden or outdoor area together to decide on suitable places for the childrens's minibeast homes to be positioned.
- Use collage to make representations of minibeast homes.

Make a ladybird shelter (pages 6-7)
- Talk about ladybirds. What can the children tell you about them?
- Look around the garden or outdoor area together to see where ladybirds like to be.
- Talk about the shape of the shelters they will be making. Where will the ladybirds be found in them do they think? Why might they like it there?
- Paint ladybirds and display them.

Get up close to minibeasts (pages 8-9)
- Who can explain how a worm moves along? Who can jump like a cricket?
- Explore minibeasts in the garden using the magnifying glasses and then draw pictures of what they have seen.

Observe snails (pages 10-11)
- Ensure children understand the importance of handling snails carefully and keeping them upright.
- What extra details can the children see using the magnifying glass?
- Who can draw the patterns seen on a snail's shell?
- Introduce the term spiral.

Make a wormery (pages 12-13)
- How long are the worms? Are they all the same? Are some fatter than others? Why might this be do they think?
- Talk about the importance of keeping the wormery dark. Encourage the children to suggest why this is important. What do they think might happen if the sides of the wormery are left uncovered?
- Talk about how the worms are good for the garden.

What's in the pond? (pages 14-15)
- Practise sitting quietly with the children. Who can stay quiet the longest?
- Record the sounds by your pond and play them back to the children later on. Which can they identify?

Pond dipping (pages 16-17)
- Talk about safety near water with the children. Draw up some safety rules and make sure everyone understands them.
- Explain what pond dipping is all about.
- Provide white or yellow trays filled with water. These colours help them see what they have caught more easily.
- Encourage the children to identify creatures of a similar type. What properties will they use to help them decide this? For example, seen only in water, seen both in and out of water, seen both in pond and stream, pond only, stream only.

A frog's life cycle (pages 18-19)
- Talk about life cycles in general. What life cycles can the children think of?
- What stages of a frog's life cycle can they describe?
- Talk through where you will get frog spawn from if your pond does not have any.
- Talk about the difference between frogspawn (round) and toad spawn (in lines).
- Introduce the frogspawn to your pond with the children. Encourage them to observe what happens to it whenever they are near it.
- Make a life cycle mural using collage materials, plotting the development of the frog's life cycle. Put dates to show each stage in development. This will help them understand about timescales.
- Encourage everyone to be a frog for drama or PE.

Make your own minibeast (pages 20-21)
- Talk about the main features of minibeasts, such as numbers of legs, wings or not, feelers and eyes.
- Explore ideas of what features the children would like to include for their minibeast. Where will they find what they need and how will they fix it together?
- Support them in exploring the garden or outdoor area to find what they need. For very young children it may be helpful to have a supply ready that you found earlier or brought in from elsewhere.
- Encourage independence but support the children in making their minibeasts where needed.
- Encourage each child to describe and show their minibeast to others.
- Take photographs for a long term record.

About this book

Each book in this series provides opportunities to enhance learning and development, supporting the four main principles of the early years foundation stage: a unique child, positive relationships, enabling environments, learning and development.

Children who are given opportunities to try, to explore, to find out about their environment and to learn through both success and error will become resilient, capable, confident and self-assured. The outdoor environment is very much an enabling environment. It provides different approaches to learning in which most children thrive, with many developing greater levels of concentration and engagement in activities than they may demonstrate indoors. The freedom of the outdoors encourages positive relationships in children with both their peers and with adults, and develops independence and inner strength. All six areas of learning and development are supported across the activities in this series. Examples of these can be seen in the charts provided at www.franklinwatts.co.uk.

The activities in this book automatically lend themselves to the introduction of new language, thinking points and questioning. They encourage exploration and investigation, both as an individual, and jointly with others. Many activities can be adapted further to meet specific learning needs.

Further information

Free downloadable activity sheets

Go to www.franklinwatts.co.uk to find these free downloadable activity sheets that accompany the activities:

• Pages 2-3: An identity chart for children to take on the minibeast hunt.
• Pages 18-19: An activity sheet for drawing a frog's life cycle.

Forest Schools

The philosophy of Forest Schools is to encourage and inspire individuals of any age through positive outdoor experiences. Go to the website to find out what happens at a Forest School, find one local to you, learn how to set one up and more.

www.forestschools.com

IMPORTANT NOTE: An adult should supervise the activities in this book, especially those near water.

Index

This edition published in 2013
by Franklin Watts

Copyright © Franklin Watts 2013

Franklin Watts
338 Euston Road
London NW1 3BH

Franklin Watts Australia
Level 17/207 Kent Street
Sydney, NSW 2000

All rights reserved.

Series editor: Sarah Peutrill
Art director: Jonathan Hair
Designer: Jane Hawkins
Photography: Chris Fairclough, unless
otherwise stated

Printed in China

The Author and Publisher would like
to thank Karen Constable, reception
class teacher at Mark First School in
Somerset, for her suggestions and help
with this series. Also thanks to the
school, especially the children, for their
enthusiasm, cooperation, and sense of
fun during the photoshoots.

Dewey number: 595.7

ISBN: 978 1 4451 1963 2

Franklin Watts is a division of
Hachette Children's Books, an
Hachette UK company.
www.hachette.co.uk

Every attempt has been made to
clear copyright. Should there be any
inadvertent omission please apply to
the publisher for rectification.

Credits:
All photography Chris Fairclough
except: Daniela Agius/istockphoto: 19c.
Alle/Shutterstock: 12t.Paul Bricknell/
FW: 2b. Martin Fowler/Shutterstock:
15b. Josiah J Garber/Shutterstock:
15t. Irin-k/Shutterstock: 6t, 7b. Eric
Isselée/Shutterstock: 3cr, 10t. Sebastian
Knight/Shutterstock: 4t. Mitzy/
Shutterstock: 18c. Mjf99/Shutterstock:
17t. Optimarc/Shutterstock: 19t.
Pakhnynshcha/Shutterstock: 17cl.
Payless Images/Shutterstock: 18t.
Picsfive/Shutterstock: 8t, 8c. pzAxe/
Shutterstock: 2t, 3c. Mauro Rodrigues/
Shutterstock: 4c. Sarah2/Shutterstock:
3tr, 8cr, 19b.SunnyS/Shutterstock: 15c.
Anke van Wyk/Shutterstock: 16t.